Options Trading:

Beginner's Guide to Make Money with Options Trading

Warren Richmond

content of this book has been derived from various sources. Please consult a licensed professional before attempting any techniques outlined in this book.

By reading this document, the reader agrees that under no circumstances are is the author responsible for any losses, direct or indirect, which are incurred as a result of the use of information contained within this document, including, but not limited to, —errors, omissions, or inaccuracies.

Table of Contents

What This Book Will Teach You

Are you curious to learn about becoming an Options Trader but unsure where to start?

Have you always wanted to make money from Options Trading, but are intimidated by the technical jargon being used?

If these questions relate well with you, then this book is for you. In this book, you will find the basic essentials to learning Trading. This book introduces readers to the "Options Trading," the in's and out, the various processes and steps involved in it.

Who this Book is for

This book contains information on how to learn Options Trading from a beginner level.

Readers who can benefit the most from the book include:

- Individuals interested in earning money from Options Trading

- Investing enthusiasts who want to learn Options Trading as another possible source of income

- Investors who would like to know more about the Trading side, beginning with Options Trading

How this Book is Organized.

This book is organized into three parts. The parts are best read in chronological order. Once you become familiar with all the steps outlined in the book, you can go directly to the techniques which apply to your current situation the best.

The three parts of the book are:

Part One outlines the essential topics on Trading and Investing, and then Options Trading in particular. The section also talks about how important it is to learn these topics as a beginner in order to form a solid foundation in doing the right steps – from introductory concepts to making your first Options Trade.

Part Two is about Risk Management and what Options Trading mistakes you can avoid in order to help minimize the chances of you losing your money. You'll learn how the process works and how to implement the steps discussed.

Part Three are the other important topics on Options Trading such as:

- Options Trading Tools
- Buying Calls
- Buying Puts
- **BONUS Chapter:** Choosing the Right Options to Trade

Introduction:

Most beginners who want to invest or trade usually go for the conventional ways of making money, such as mutual funds, stocks, bonds, Exchange Traded Funds, or real estate. You may have heard about Options but don't quite understand what they are or how they work. You may have bought into the prevailing view that this form of trading is simply too risky.

However, this book will show you that Options trading is a simple way that you can also make money. All you need for Options trading is the right knowledge so that you can better understand how it all works.

When it comes to trading in Options, you have a wide range of choices and strategies available, depending on what you want to achieve. Options trading may seem a bit complex at first, but once you master a couple of key strategies, you will be good to go.

This book will teach you the basics of Options trading in a way that will allow you to understand in a clear and concise manner. You will discover the benefits that come with trading in Options compared to the other financial instruments. We will also walk you through how to make that crucial first trade so that you set up a platform for your future success.

The majority of beginner traders make some costly mistakes, and some of the biggest ones are discussed in this book. It is important that you recognize where the potential pitfalls are so that you minimize your chances of losing money.

Options have their own risks, just like stocks, bonds, and mutual funds. Due to its high level of leverage, Options trading can be very risky, but that is why you need this book to teach you the ins and outs. There is no need to miss out on the profit potential of options because of fear. Proper education is the key thing, and once you learn about how to manage risks and use different types of tools effectively, you will become a more efficient trader.

The goal of this book is to unravel the mystery that is Options trading so that beginners can learn what it is all about. Consider this book a door-opener since it is written to pave the way for you to motivate you to learn more about Options. As long as you are willing to learn continuously, you are going to be a successful Options trader.

Chapter 1: Trading & Investing Basics Explained

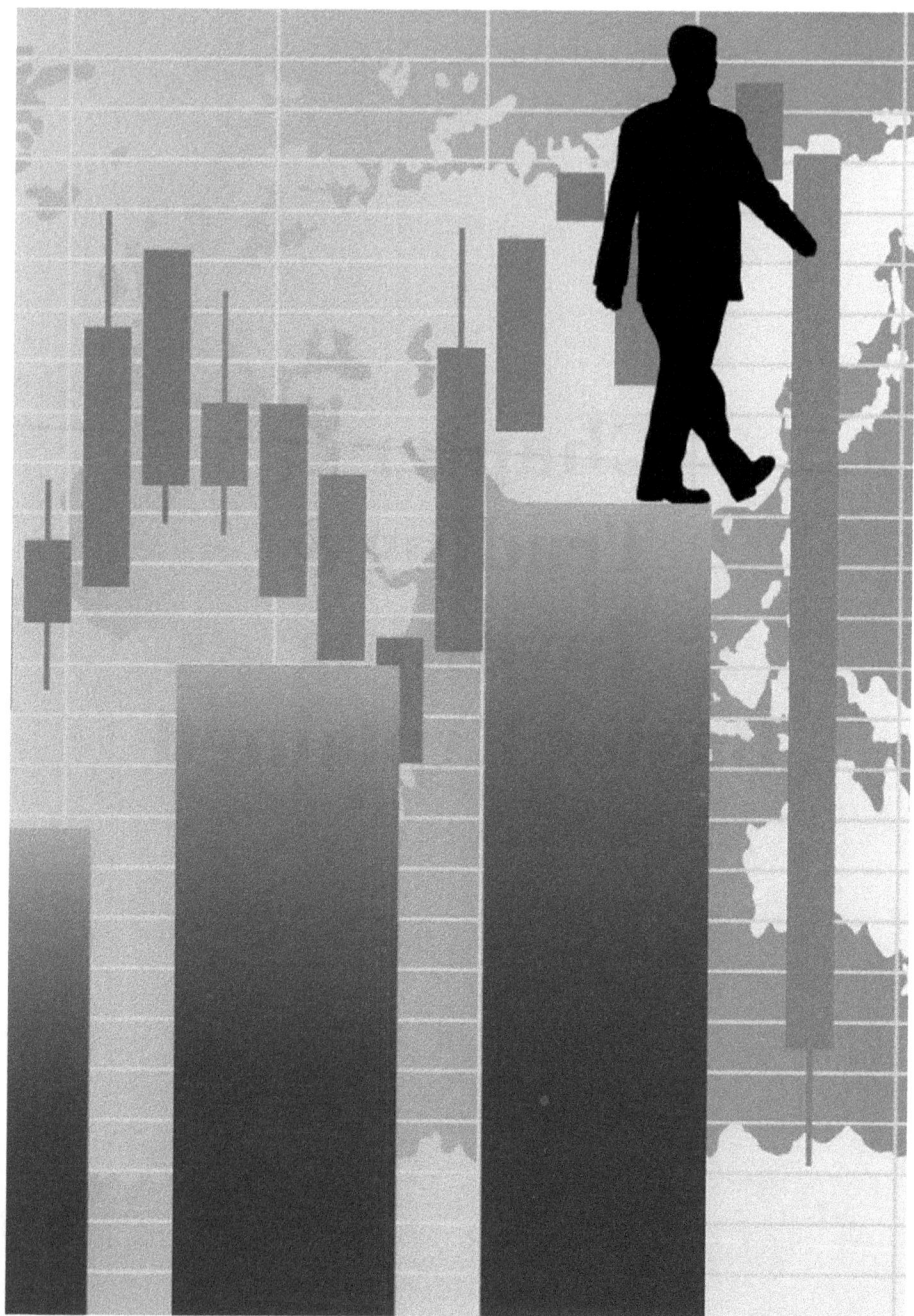

1.1 Background of Trading and Investing

The simplest way to define trading is that it is the buying and selling of products and services between parties. In most cases, the medium of exchange is money, but it can also involve virtual currency or direct exchange of goods for other goods. The network that facilitates trade is known as a market. Trade originally started through bartering, where goods and services were exchanged for other goods and services. Later on, it grew to incorporate precious metals.

Investing, on the other hand, is aimed at building wealth over a long period of time, usually years or decades. It involves buying and holding an asset with the expectation that it will generate a return or increase in value in the future. This return may come in the form of dividends, interest, or selling the asset at a higher price.

Types of Trading

There are several different categories of trading. In terms of volume, there is retail trading and wholesale trading. In terms of the medium of exchange, there is barter trading, virtual currency trading, and cash trading. In terms of financial assets, there is stock trading, Forex trading, options trading, futures trading, and commodities trading. However, since this a book aimed at imparting financial knowledge, we shall focus exclusively on options trading from here on out.

Historical Basis of Trading and Investing

Trading began in prehistoric times, more than 150, 000 years ago, when humans started bartering. Money had not yet been invented so traders simply exchanged the goods they had for other goods that they wanted. With time, barter trade evolved to include precious metals. Trading was greatly enhanced and simplified when money was invented.

Investing began with the Code of Hammurabi, which established a legitimate structure for investing, around 1700 B.C. This code set up a mechanism for defining the rights of the debtor and creditor with regard to the pledging of collateral for land. By the 1900s, speculators had risen up. These were people who bought all kinds of high-risk securities. Later on, the term investment came to refer to the buying of low-risk or conservative securities.

1.2 Benefits of Learning the Basics of Trading

- Explain why learning the basic of Trading is important to a person who wants to succeed in this field.

You are probably itching to dive right into the nitty-gritty details of how to trade in options. That is commendable. Passion will take you far.

However, it is even more important to first learn the basics of trading. This one step will have a greater impact on whether you achieve success as a trader or not. As a beginner who may be interested in becoming a successful trader, it is important for you to learn all the fundamentals regarding how a regular market works and the tools and strategies required. It is a well-known fact that becoming an experienced trader requires extensive knowledge on the basics of trading.

Every trade requires a willing buyer and a willing seller. They must both have something that they are willing to give up in exchange for another item that they desire more. There has to be a price that is suitable for both parties. They also must agree on the medium of exchange. All these components must be in place for trading to occur. By learning the basics of trading, you are better placed to understand how to trade and how to maximize your profit margin.

The benefits of learning the basics of trading include:

- You will be able to make more informed decisions based on well-researched information.

- You will learn what obligations both the buyer and seller have when it comes to exchanging of goods, services, and money.

- You will get to understand how trading began and its fundamental structure.

- You will be able to make profits regardless of whether the market is up or down.

- It makes your entry into the market much smoother.

- You will learn how to negotiate for goods and services for a fair price.

- You will know how to develop the most appropriate trading strategy for your business.

- You will know which aspects of trade to focus your business on, depending on market responses.

- You will learn how to use marketing strategies to draw buyers to your goods.

1.3 How Basic Trading Works

In this section, we want to talk about the steps of basic trading:

- Determine the need in the market. Ask yourself what gaps are in the market or where the demand is.

- Determine whether you already have the goods or services the market requires. If not, then acquire them.

- Find a willing buyer who is interested in the product or service.

- Set a price for your product or service. A smart trader always leaves room for negotiation.

- Hand over the good or service to the other party in exchange for money.

CHAPTER SUMMARY:

1. Trading and investing are two terms that are usually used interchangeably but are totally different. Trading is the buying and selling of products and services

between parties, usually involving money. However, it can also involve virtual currency or bartering.

2. Investing is buying financial instruments with the goal of holding onto them for many years in order to take advantage of compounding and reap yearly profits and dividends.

3. There are several different types of trade cutting across various categories. In this book, we focus specifically on options trading.

4. Trading began around 150,000 years ago with barter trade being the main means of trade. Investing is a concept that came to the scene much later on. It started with the Code of Hammurabi way back in 1700 BC.

5. While passion and enthusiasm are great to have when you are a new trader, there is no substitute for knowledge of the fundamentals of trading. It is important to learn the basics of trading in order to gain a firm foundation for making all your trading decisions. This will enable you to boost your chances of trading successfully and making consistent profits.

6. The steps to trading are quite easy. Once you know what the market demands and put the supply in place, you are well positioned to find a buyer and negotiate the best price.

YOUR QUICK START ACTION STEP:

This chapter has just introduced you to the basics of trading but is definitely not exhaustive. There is still a lot of information that you need to learn. The good news is that there are a lot of other resources out there that can help you become a better trader. We recommend that you take the time to visit *www.tradestation.com* for more information.

Chapter 2: Options Trading Essentials

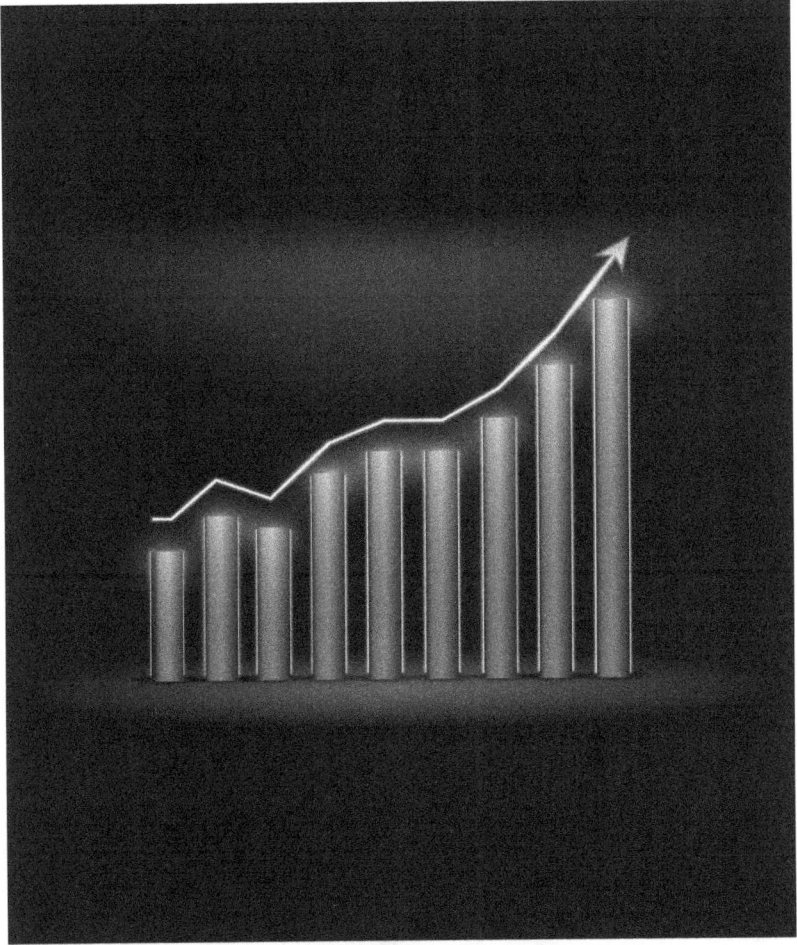

2.1 What is Options Trading?

In order to understand options trading, we must first get to know what we mean by an "option." An option is a financial contract that gives the owner/holder the right, but not the obligation, to purchase or sell an underlying asset at a specified price on or before a specified date. Once the given date expires, the contract ceases to exist.

The underlying asset can be any of the financial instruments that are traded in the market, for example, stocks, indices, mutual funds, ETFs, and so on. For purposes of consistency, we will assume throughout the book that the underlying asset is a stock.

The price that is specified in an options contract is referred to as the *strike price*. This price may be set according to the market price of the underlying asset on the day that the options contract was taken out.

The date that is specified in the contract is referred to as the *expiration* date. This is the date by which the buyer of the options should have exercised their right.

So, let's try to simplify this further. When trading in options, you are essentially trading a contract, and there must be two parties involved. The seller has an obligation to sell the options to or purchase the options from the buyer upon the buyer's request. The buyer (or holder) has the right to buy or sell the underlying asset, but in order to acquire this right, they have to pay the seller a premium.

There are generally two types of options: *Call* options and *Put* options. A call option gives the owner the right to buy the underlying asset at the strike price. The seller usually issues a call option when they think that the price of the underlying asset will drop below the prevailing market price. In other words, the seller feels that they are better off pegging the strike price now so that even if the price drops in the future, they will be able to prevent losses.

A put option gives the owner the right to sell the underlying asset at the strike price. A put option is usually exercised when the holder of the options contract thinks that the price of the underlying asset will go up in the future. In other words, the holder of the options contract has the right to sell their options at a strike price that is higher than the prevailing market value, thus earning them a profit.

Every time an option is exercised, the buyer pays a cost equivalent to the strike price plus the premium. If the expiration date passes and the options have not been exercised, then the buyer forfeits the premium to the seller. This premium acts as a form of income to the seller and is considered a loss to the buyer.

The History of Options Trading

Throughout history, there has always been some form of options contracts. The Greek philosopher Thales of Miletus is considered to be the first well-known options buyer. After hearing of a prediction that the olive harvest would be bigger than normal the coming season, he went ahead to purchase the right to use several olive presses during the spring season. When the large harvest came in, he exercised his options and hired out the presses at a higher price than he had paid for the options.

In the 1690s, puts and calls became popular in London. In 19th Century America, privileges were sold over the counter, and specialized dealers offered calls and puts on shares. The strike price was fixed according to the market price when the option was bought. The expiration date was usually set three months after the purchase.

In real estate, call options were used to assemble large tracts of land from different owners. For example, a real estate developer would pay for the right to purchase a number of adjacent plots, but would not be under any obligation to do so unless he could purchase every plot in the area of interest. Even film producers normally buy the rights to turn a book into a movie, though they are not obligated to do so.

2.2 Importance of Building a Basic Foundation in Options Trading

As a beginner in options trading, you are probably thinking that since options are some kind of complex financial instrument, then you need to focus on intricate strategies in order to become successful. However, you will be surprised to discover that building the basic foundation will do more for your success than any other action you take.

The truth is that learning the basics will help you become more effective when generating income or hedging against risk. If you focus on the fundamentals, you can even do both at the same time. Yes, there are many complex strategies in options trading, but as a new trader, the most straightforward ones are the ones that will help you develop the right foundation.

More than 90% of new traders who plunge into the options market end up losing their capital. Most beginners jump in head first without realizing the importance of first building up your knowledge of the fundamentals of options trading. In options trading, there are numerous benefits but there are also some risks that you have to learn how to manage. The more knowledge you acquire and put into practice, the better your chances of succeeding.

In summary, here are the benefits:

- Once you understand the fundamentals, you can use that as a launching pad for gaining further education.

- You can learn many of the virtually unlimited possibilities that are available when trading in the options market.

- You will realize that the options market has diverse strategies that work both in bearish as well as bullish markets.

- You will be able to determine whether options trading can be a career or simply a way to make passive income.

- You can learn how to combine options and stocks to reduce risk and increase your profit potential.

- You will be able to preserve your capital by avoiding silly options trading mistakes.

2.3 How Options Trading Works

In this section, we want to describe to you in a basic way how trading in options works:

1. Assume you see a company that is performing well. You think that its stocks will increase in value in the near future, so you decide to invest in its stocks.

2. Instead of buying its shares outright, you buy an options contract for the underlying stock. Buying options don't require as much capital as it would cost to buy the stocks directly. NB: Every options contract represents 100 shares.

3. You pay the seller of the stock options a premium (less amount than total capital required) to hold the stocks for you until a specified date when you will come and pay a predetermined (strike) price. At this point, you don't own the stocks; you simply own a contract that gives you the right to buy the stocks. You are under no obligation to buy the stocks in the future.

4. If the value of the company's stocks goes up, then you can exercise your right and buy the stocks at the predetermined strike price, which is less than current market value. Of course, this must be

done before the expiry of the specified date.

5. You can then hold on to the stocks and wait for the price to keep rising, or cash in immediately to make a profit.

6. Alternatively, let's go back to Step 4 and consider what would happen if the value of the company's stocks didn't go up as you had predicted, and actually went down. If you exercise your right, you will end up paying more than the prevailing market price. However, you are under no obligation to buy the stocks. So you choose to let the contract expire and walk away. You limit your loss to the premium you paid the seller.

This is a simplified version of how a call option works.

CHAPTER SUMMARY:

1. An option is a financial contract that gives the owner/holder the right, but not the obligation, to purchase or sell an underlying asset at a specified price on or before a specified date. Once the given date expires, the contract ceases to exist.

2. There are generally two types of options: *Call* options and *Put* options. A call option gives the owner the right to buy the underlying asset at the strike price. A put option gives the owner the right to sell the underlying asset at the strike price.

3. Options trading began in ancient Greece when Thales of Miletus bought the rights to use olive presses in the off-season and then hired them out at a profit during harvest season. It has evolved to now involve shares, real estate, and even book rights.

4. It is important to first focus on learning the basics of options trading to become a successful trader. For beginners, the simplest strategies are the most effective.

5. Options trading work in a logical and effective manner. Follow the steps properly and you will be able to minimize risks and increase your profit potential.

YOUR QUICK START ACTION STEP:

This chapter has just introduced you to the essentials of options trading, but it is definitely not exhaustive. There is still a lot of information that you need to learn about how to trade in options. The good news is that there are a lot of other resources out there that can help you become a better options trader. We recommend that you take the time to visit *www.optionsguide.com* for more information.

Chapter 3:
The Benefits of
Options Trading

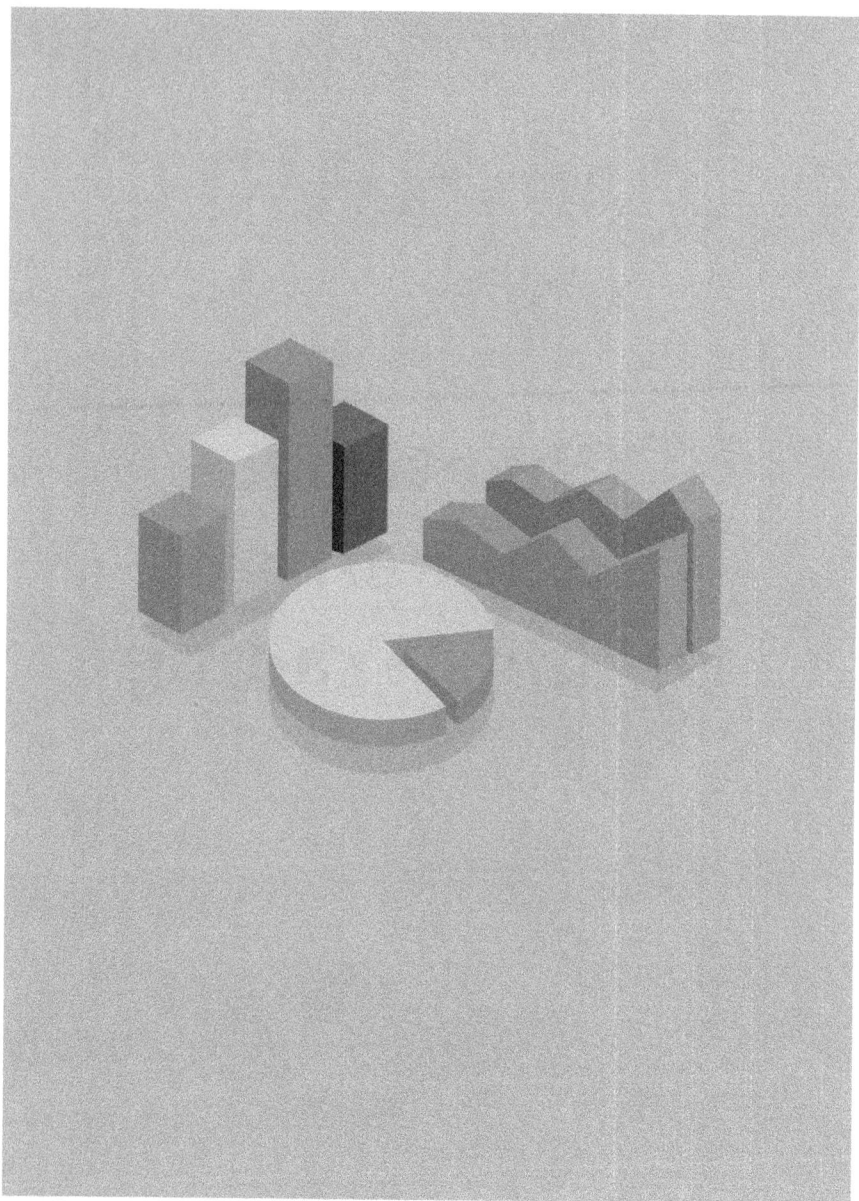

3.1 Focusing on Options Trading

It should be clear by now that focusing on options trading has its benefits. For those who are interested in options trading, whether as a career or for investment purposes, trading options can be a very lucrative proposition.

Options can be traded in a retirement account. This is an appealing strategy that can grow and hedge your portfolio over the long term. If you are looking for diversification with little capital, then options trading should be part of your primary focus. Options are cheaper than buying stocks outright, which means that new investors can easily take advantage of the many opportunities that options allow.

The liquidity and efficiency of options markets should also motivate you to focus on options trading. Options allow you to capitalize on stock price movements at a rate that is much higher than that of the underlying stocks.

Most traders have often believed that focusing on penny stocks and low dollar stocks is the way to go, but if you consider the conservative and logical trading approach that options offer, you quickly realize how wrong that belief is. There are so many strategies and a wide risk tolerance range when it comes to trading in options. No matter what style you choose to adopt, or your level of risk appetite, you can always trade options and still reap a profit.

3.2 Importance of Options Trading

Most people who are starting out, whether as career options traders or merely interested in making options trades for money, tend to become distracted by all the information that they read on the Internet. They tend to be impatient because they know they can make money very quickly.

However, to become a successful trader, you must understand the importance of options trading. You need to realize that options trading must involve the right strategies and outlook to work together to boost your chances of succeeding in the market.

Options trading involve creating a trading plan which guides how you enter, exit and manage your money. Though it takes some time to develop and test the plan, it is worth it.

Options trading also ensure that your trades are done professionally and business-like. You should consider yourself like a small business owner so that you take the entire process seriously. You shouldn't take unnecessary risks that will erode your trading capital.

Through all the research that is involved in options trading, you quickly get to learn how the market operates. This boosts your focus on acquiring more knowledge so that you are always on top of trends and patterns that may affect your profits and losses.

Understanding the importance of options trading is the first step toward developing your strategies and converting it into a viable trading business. You must commit yourself to developing the patience and commitment necessary for success.

Benefits of Options Trading

- Leverage – With options, you can use a number of different strategies in order to reap maximum profit. You basically invest very little of your own capital and end up reaping great gains.

- Hedging – This means minimizing your exposure to losses. It is done by establishing a position in the options market in order to offset your exposure to volatile prices in the stock market. Hedging is a great way to protect your portfolio.

- Lower commissions – Options trading is cheaper than stock trading because there is stiff competition among online options brokerages. You can take advantage of the discounts on offer to keep your trading costs at a minimum.

- Limited risk and high potential for success.

- Options provide an income (premium) every time you sell your right to buy stocks at a specified price.

- It doesn't matter which the direction the market moves. You can always make a profit even when the market moves down or sideways.

- Executing options transactions is quick, which means that you can cash in at any time. You will have more time to reinvest your cash than you would with your money tied up in shares.

3.3 How to Stay Focused When Trading Options

Every options trader needs to maintain a high level of focus when trading. There are particular factors and attributes that can help you do that. They include:

1. Adequate capitalization – While it is true that you require little capital to enter the market, thanks to its leverage power, it would be wise to ensure that you have enough capital. To maintain your focus, you need to make sure that a few losing trades do not wipe out all your capital.

2. Low-risk appetite – Successful options traders only trade when they see a low-risk-high-reward option. It's only the rookies who try to hit a home run every single time.

3. Patience – focused options traders are patient and trade only when they discern that the odds are stacked in their favor. You need to learn to wait as you focus on the bigger picture.

4. Trading plan – This is the first thing you need to have before you even open a trading account. Write it down and follow it no matter what your emotions tell you.

5. Risk management plan – This will keep you from trading when you don't have the money for it. Options trading is more than just looking at the potential profits. There are risks involved, too.

CHAPTER SUMMARY:

1. Focusing on options trading has numerous benefits. It is a great way to diversify and hedge your investment portfolio. There is little cash required to start as a new trader. The market is always liquid, which means you can sell your options and exit with your cash quickly. Any style or risk level of trading can be successful in an options market.

2. If you want to become a successful options trader, then you must learn the ins and outs of options trading. There is no escaping the fact that you have to learn first and invest later.

3. There are many benefits to trading in options. Though it may be a bit complex when you start out, you can make money easily and fast, as long as you have taken the time to focus on the fundamentals of options trading.

4. Maintaining your focus while trading in options is critical. There are specific skills and factors that can help you be successful as a trader. These include proper capitalization, low risk-tolerance, patience, creating a trading plan, and maintaining a risk management plan.

YOUR QUICK START ACTION STEP:

There is a lot of online information that can help you maintain your focus on stock trading. There are websites that cater to options traders, even beginners. You can find many relevant sources that will guide you along and you can even start trading using a virtual platform if you wish.

Chapter 4: Options Trading Success: What to Look Out For

4.1 Factors Determining Options Trading Success

As someone who is interested in options trading, what does success mean to you? What do you think it takes to become a successful options trader?

This question may seem easy to answer. Most beginner traders would simply say that it's the amount of money you make that defines whether you are successful or not. To such people, success would mean coming up with an options trading strategy that enables you to have an edge over the market time and time again. So, does this mean that taking a class about options trading will give you all the tools you need to become a successful trader?

Most beginner traders wrongly assume that learning to trade is like reading for an exam. You immerse yourself in books and then wait to get all the answers correct. However, trading is more similar to learning a sport. Nobody starts playing football today and expects to become the best player after just a few months of studying the game.

What is the point being made here? It's really simple. A trader requires time and experience before they can become successful at what they do. Think of options trading as more of a marathon rather than a sprint.

Another factor that determines success in options trading is your way of thinking. Let me tell you a big secret about trading options – sooner or later, you will lose some money! The biggest difference between a successful trader and one who struggles to meet their goals is how they handle losses. Trading in options isn't a test, so don't beat yourself up whenever you make a few bad trades. Just make sure that you keep the mistakes (and losses) to a minimum.

How you allow your emotions to control you when you trade, especially after being hit by consecutive losses, is a huge factor. It is very common for new traders to abandon their preferred trading strategy to look for another one simply because they feel that the previous one doesn't work. To be successful in trading options, you will have to learn how to be patient and not take trades personally.

The truth is that trading options should be treated like a business. You need to develop the patience and persistence and take the time to learn. To be a successful options trader, you will have to develop the kind of consistency that the great traders of the past and present generation have produced. Read their trading history and you will realize that they failed many times. The only reason why we still talk about them is because they kept at it until they learned to produce consistent profits.

Benefits of Options Trading

There are a number of benefits to trading in options. They include:

- Options allow you to leverage whatever little capital you may have.

- Options offer greater flexibility in decision-making than stocks.

- Options enable you to customize your risk level according to your comfort level.

- Options can earn you a profit via speculation.

- Options can be an effective hedge for your portfolio.

- Options will still generate a profit regardless of the direction of the market.

4.2 Parameters for Successful Options Trading

When it comes to determining which parameters can influence the success of an options trade, look no further than these factors: Fundamental analysis, implied and historical volatility, charting, and many other options valuation strategies. These are all important parameters to consider. However, the overriding parameter to focus on when trading options must be liquidity.

Why is it important to be armed with this information? The simple truth is that your success depends on it! The vast majority of new traders barely bother to learn the fundamentals of what will affect their earnings. You cannot afford to dive into the options market without first getting a firm understanding of the factors that will define whether you make a profit or leave with a loss.

Knowledge is power, and in the options trading world, that power can make you wealthy in the long term. These parameters need to be at your fingertips so that every time you trade in options, you will have analyzed your position and be confident of winning.

The first group of parameters mentioned above is all necessary when trading in options, but they all point to short-term success. Liquidity or the bid/ask spread, affects the cost of implementing a trading position. If the market is illiquid, you will find it difficult to achieve success in the long term.

Here are a few benefits of staying informed about the parameters for successful options trading:

- Knowledge of parameters helps in evaluation of the worthiness of a potential trade.

- It helps you pick those options that will bring a good rate of return.

- It helps you take trading positions that won't eat into your profits.

- It helps you achieve consistent and profitable results.

- It helps you focus on liquidity, which is the true test of a profitable market.

4.3 How to Measure Success in Options Trading

The question that needs to be answered here is, "What is the true measure of success when it comes to trading options?"

1. Developing strict money management rules. You might have a winning percentage, but if your losses outweigh your winners, you will lose money overall.

2. Understanding your risk and trading according to what you can afford to lose. If you take 10% on every trade you make, 10 consecutive losses will wipe

you out. Determine your risk tolerance, and take into account the power of leverage.

3. Spending a fixed amount of your capital on each trade you make. It is always tempting to want to buy more contracts after experiencing a string of positive results. However, such kind of confidence can lead you to toss your plan out of the window, which is a recipe for disaster.

4. Trading in a calculated way. In other words, instead of being greedy or cherry-picking your trades just adhere to your trading plan and money management rules.

CHAPTER SUMMARY:

1. Defining success when options trading is more than just looking at what strategy to use to make the most money in the short term. There are specific characteristics and attributes successful traders have that make them come out on top. Success requires time, patience, persistence, experience, and consistency in learning.

2. There are numerous benefits to trading in options. These include leverage of low

capital, flexibility in making decisions, ease of customization, hedging, and high profits.

3. There are certain parameters that you need to take seriously for successful stock trading. These include liquidity of the market, fundamental analysis, charting, and volatility. Of all these, liquidity is the secret to success.

4. Measuring success when trading in options involves having strict money management rules. This can be achieved in three ways – understanding your risk, trading a fixed amount consistently, and being calculating rather than a greedy or picky trader.

YOUR QUICK START ACTION STEP:

At this point, we suggest that you do some basic research to identify a couple of traders who managed to make it big through options trading. As you read about their stories, take a pen and notepad and jot down some of the strategies they used. You should focus on any tips that you can learn and practice right now.

Chapter 5: Making Your First Options Trade

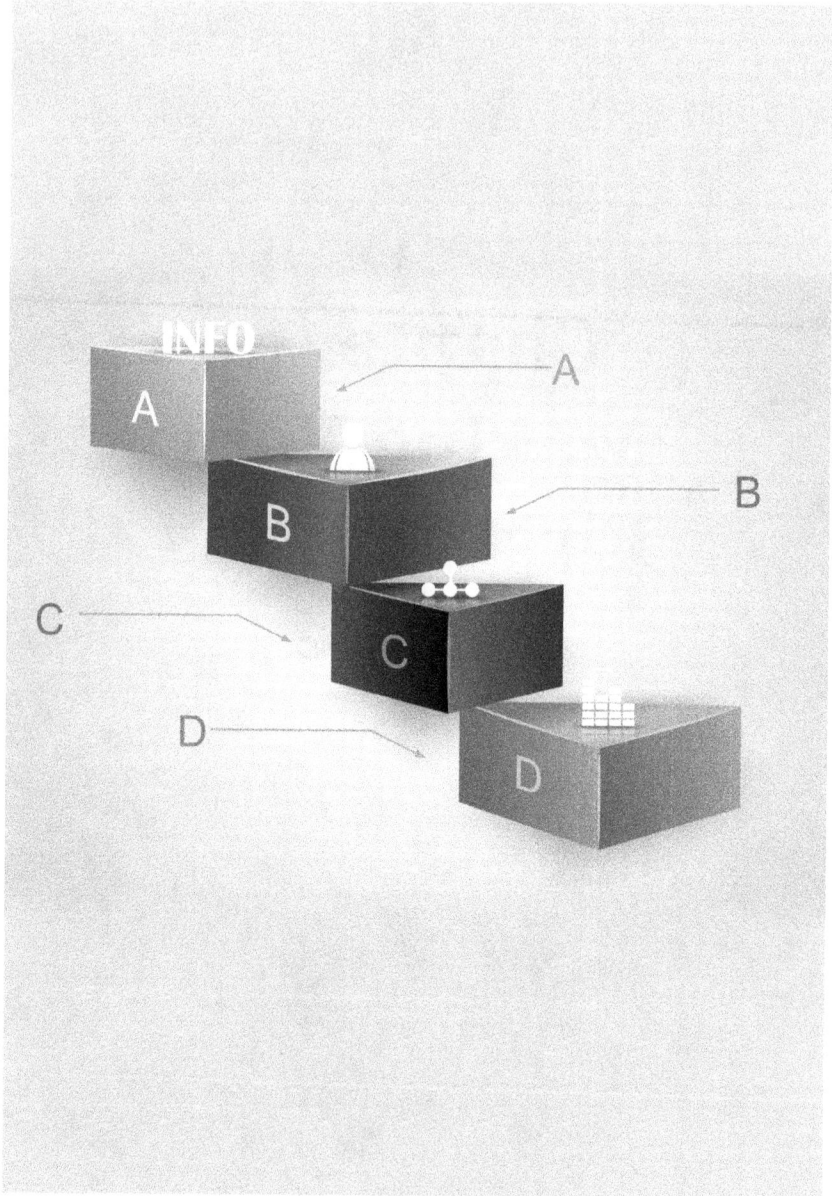

5.1 Factors to Consider

Now that you believe you know enough about options trading, you are probably contemplating making the first options trade. This can be very exhilarating! You are excited and can't wait to begin stacking that paper.

However, things aren't that easy. You need to be careful how you go about it so that you do not place your money at risk. You must ensure that you follow the right procedure so that you avoid making costly mistakes. In this chapter, we cover some of the specific steps that can lead you to make your first successful options trade.

But before we look at how to make an options trade for the first time, let us examine the particular aspects of the options trading process that every new trader should keep in mind. This is vital information so make sure that you understand the details before you begin trading.

Firstly, you need to be aware that there are many different factors that affect whether your trade will earn you a profit or not. Most new traders are so excited about making their first trade that all they focus on is buying calls and expecting to reap rewards when the price of the underlying stock rises. In order to earn a profit, you must consider the many factors that influence the price of an option.

Secondly, you need to be aware of the history of the stock price. You may be bullish about the price of a particular stock (you expect it to rise), yet can you estimate by how much the price will change? You have to set reasonable expectations, and this can only be possible by examining the just how volatile the price of that stock has been in the past. You will be terribly disappointed if you buy $50 call options for an expiration date of 90 days, yet that particular stock moves an average of $0.05 each day! It would make more sense to go for options whose stock price moves $0.5 every day.

Thirdly, consider the strike price when buying options. Most traders tend to buy OTM options simply because they are cheap and believe that stand a better chance of making a profit if they own a lot of options. This is not the lottery! You need to buy options based on the volatility of the stock price. Make sure that your options have a high probability of being in-the-money before expiration.

Finally, never buy options expecting to hold them until the contract expires. Know this – you are handling wasting assets, so be ready to offload them as soon as possible. Don't get greedy and hold on for too long, as you target a higher profit. It is unwise to develop a love affair with your options, so keep your emotions out of the game!

The steps and recommendations that have been outlined above in this chapter have been proven to help new traders break into any options market and make successful trades. Remember that as an options trader, you need to develop a system that will always be there to guide you. If you follow it, you won't regret it.

5.2 Why You Need These Steps

The steps that will be outlined in the section below are fundamental to every new options trader. If you intend to buy options for the first time, do not make the mistake of buying calls without considering all the underlying factors involves. You have to take the time to examine volatility of the stock price with regards to the past.

Most new traders treat options trading like the lottery; they buy a lot of cheap OTM calls thinking that at least one of them will make them a handsome profit. This is a terrible strategy that won't help you in the long run. Options are supposed to make you a profit, but if you find yourself losing money time and again, it may be time to rethink your steps.

That is why you need to take the time to learn all the steps required to make a successful first options trade. Therefore, be diligent at all times and follow the right procedure.

There are some specific benefits that you get from following these steps. They include:

- You learn to become aware of all the underlying factors that affect your profit-earning potential.

- You learn how to dig into the historical background of stocks and their average move prices.

- You focus on buying options that are likely to be in the money rather than simply going for the cheap ones.

- You position yourself to know how much to pay for available options.

- You avoid wasting time and holding on to your options until they expire.

5.3 Steps for Trading in Options for the First Time

1. Find a good brokerage by researching widely and seeking out referrals from more experienced traders.

2. Decide whether you want to trade with an online or offline brokerage. Online brokerages are the preferred mode of options trading.

3. Open a trading account with your options brokerage. You can choose to open a margin account or a cash account.

4. With a margin account, you will be able to use your existing stocks or long-term options as security when getting a loan from the brokerage to make extra purchases.

5. With a cash account, you don't have the option of getting a loan. You simply rely on the money in your account.

6. Make the minimum deposit requested by the brokerage. The amount usually depends on the type of trading account and your brokerage firm's policies. Cash accounts require significantly lower deposit amounts than margin accounts.

CHAPTER SUMMARY:

1. There are some fundamental aspects of options trading that every beginner should learn before they engage in their first trade. Firstly, consider all the factors that influence the price of an option. Don't just focus on buying calls and waiting for the price to go up. Secondly, keep your expectations

realistic by exploring the history of the underlying stock price. Thirdly, consider the probability of your stock price being in-the-money before expiration rather than buying options because they are cheap. Finally, always be prepared to sell your options before expiration.

2. It is unwise to rush into stock trading without following the right procedure. In fact, there are several benefits you gain from simply doing things the right way. You will end up saving yourself a lot of money, time, and stress.

3. The steps for options trading start with ensuring that you have a strong financial foundation. Once you open an account with a good online brokerage, you should identify the type of trading account you want. Then deposit the minimum amount required. Finally, go to the broker's website and fill in your order.

YOUR QUICK START ACTION STEP:

You now know exactly how to make that first options trade, so go ahead and try it. You can easily sign up for a virtual trading account with a reputable brokerage. Start practicing your options trades as soon as possible so that you learn how to become a successful trader. Remember, practice makes perfect!

Chapter 6: Options Trading Mistakes: What to Avoid

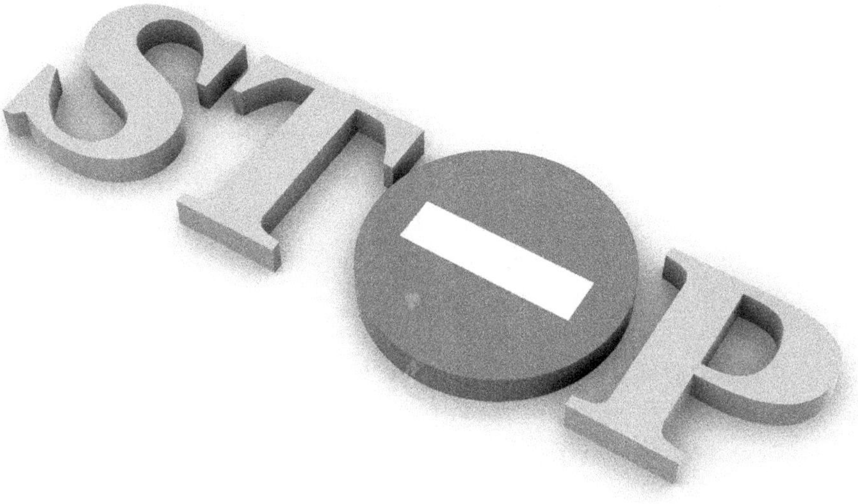
STOP

6.1 Overview

Every rookie makes a mistake. That is just part of the learning process. However, something must be done about it. With over 10 years' experience in trading securities, especially options trading, I have noticed that new traders and investors keep on repeating some specific mistakes over and over again.

The truth is that trading in options is not a straightforward process. It is not like trading stocks, where you just buy, hold for a short time, and then sell for a profit. Trading in options has a certain level of complexity that beginners must first acknowledge. The reason why new traders are always repeating these mistakes is because they fail to clearly understand how options work.

It is not just about correctly anticipating the direction of price movements. You also have to be accurate with the timing. An option is not as liquid as a stock, which means that you will have to incur higher costs due to the larger spreads between the bid and ask price. New traders also tend to be ignorant of the fact that the value of an option incorporates numerous variables that influence its final outcome.

These are just some of the reasons that explain why the following ten options trading mistakes are common with new traders.

Top 10 Options Trading Mistakes

- **Buying Out-of-The-Money (OTM) call options from the beginning.** Most beginners use the buy low sell high strategy they are used to in equity trading. Testing the waters with this strategy will lead to consistent losses.

- **Adopting a one-strategy-fits-all style of trading.** Most new traders have an all-purpose strategy that they use regardless of market conditions.

- **Failing to have a clear exit plan before the expiration date.** One of the most priceless pieces of advice you can learn is to never trade with your emotions. In other words, create a plan, and stick to it.

- **Compromising your tolerance for risk.** It is common, even among veteran traders, to be tempted to "double-up" to make up for past losses. It is easy to compromise your personal rules and trading plan when a trade moves against you yet you insist on maintaining the same trade option. This may work for stocks but not necessarily for options.

- **Trading illiquid options.** Liquidity refers to how fast you can buy or sell your assets without causing a considerable movement in prices. In a liquid market, there are always ready buyers and sellers. If you trade options for a company whose stock rarely moves, then you will end up with an extremely wide bid-ask spread. This is never a good idea.

- **Failing to buy back your short options.** Waiting too long to buy back your short options just because you want to be cheap will end up costing you more money. Most traders don't want to pay commission fees or are hoping that somehow they can squeeze some extra profit from the trade.

- **Failing to take into account dividend payments dates as part of your strategy.** By not factoring in these dates, you run the risk of being assigned earnings that end up making options contracts more expensive, for both calls and puts.

- **Failing to have a strategy for early assignment.** The majority of new traders rarely consider that they may get assigned. This becomes a very emotionally jarring experience, especially if you are using long or short spreads.

- **"Legging" into spread trades.** Most traders take unnecessary risks by buying a call and then attempting to "leg in" another call, just to eke out a higher price from the second leg.

- **Not trading options based on indices.** Unlike stocks, which can plummet due to some unexpected news affecting a company, index options never fluctuate too much. If you fail to use index options when performing neutral trades, you will definitely feel the full impact of uncertainty in the market.

6.2 Importance of Avoiding Mistakes

Every trader who chooses to trade in options does so because they want to make money. The mistakes highlighted above can be extremely costly in the long run. You need to be aware of these potential pitfalls and avoid them as much as you can if you want to succeed as an options trader.

If you can minimize the mistakes, you can gain greater control over your risks and rewards. If you keep stumbling along due to the same mistakes, you won't last very long in options trading.

Here are a few benefits of avoiding these mistakes:

- You will be able to preserve your capital and learn better strategies in the process.

- You will be able to earn income without taking on undue opportunity risks.

- You will become more flexible when it comes to choosing the right strategy according to prevailing market conditions.

- You will be able to minimize losses, make consistent profits, and enjoy your sleep since you won't be trading based on emotions.

- You will lower your cost of doing business.

- You will be able to maximize your profits with lower risk.

- You will be able to avoid paying more money for calls and puts contracts.

- You will minimize the impact that unforeseen news has on the market.

6.3 Steps on How to Avoid Mistakes

1. When you first begin to trade options, consider adopting a "covered call" strategy. Start by selling OTM calls on stocks that you own already.

2. Stay open to learning as many new strategies as possible. Buying spreads is a great way to learn how to profit from on diverse market conditions.

3. Create an exit plan and follow through on it. This allows you to develop a consistent trading pattern that reduces worry and risk.

4. Learn how to cut your losses early when options trades don't go your way.

5. Always be prepared and willing to purchase your short options back as soon as possible.

6. Keep track of the dates for issuing dividends and other earnings for your underlying stock. Avoid those options contracts that have pending dividends.

7. Trade your spreads as one trade instead of buying one call and then trying to time the sale of another call.

8. Consider adopting trading strategies that involve short spreads on indices. This will enable you to stay neutral when the markets are impacted by negative news.

CHAPTER SUMMARY:

1. There are some mistakes that are more common than others, especially among beginner traders. This is due to the complexity of options trading.

2. Most beginners make mistakes repeatedly because they fail to take the time to learn how the options market works. They simply look at the direction of movement of the prices but ignore the spreads, the costs, and the underlying variables involved.

3. There are 10 common mistakes that new traders make. These mistakes can be avoided by simply ensuring that you consider all the factors required to make a profitable trade.

4. Jumping in head first will cost you a lot of money. The best strategy you can have is to learn how to avoid the silly mistakes that everyone else is making.

5. Avoiding options trading mistakes requires learning as many strategies as possible. Keep your mind open and be patient enough to understand the ins and outs of the market.

YOUR QUICK START ACTION STEP:

It is very important that you understand the 10 mistakes highlighted in this chapter. There is no point in rushing forward to trade options only to trip and fall due to a mistake you were warned about. Always be conscious of these pitfalls when you make your next options trade.

Chapter 7:
Options Trading Risk Management

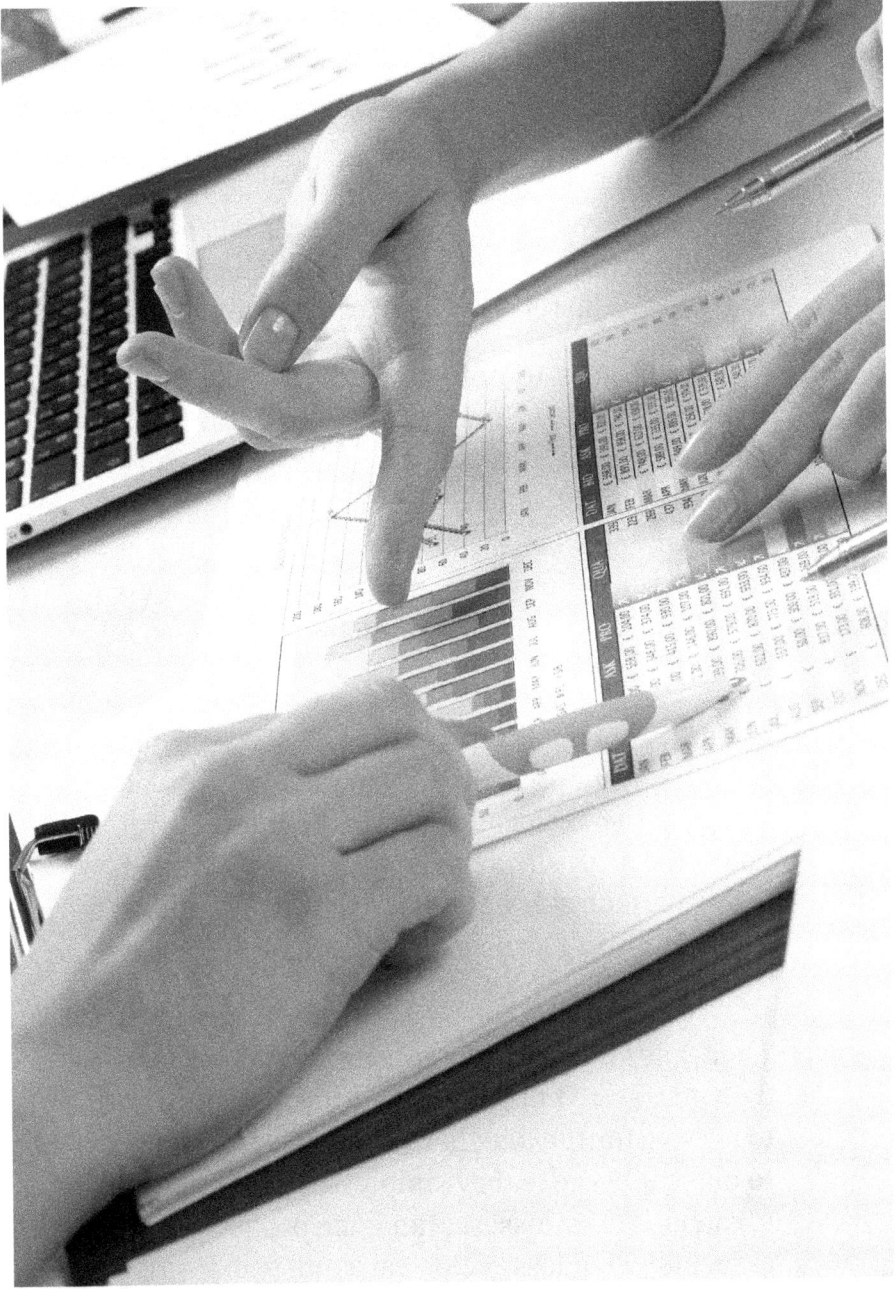

7.1 Risk Management Defined

Risk management can be defined as the identification and evaluation of risks with the aim of formulating strategies to minimize these risks and maximize the profits. Trading in options always involves the two elements of risk and return. If the risks are high, then in most cases the returns are likely to be high.

When it comes to options trading, there is no escaping the fact that you are going to have to face some risks. Most new traders simply have to learn that trading in options is nothing like stock trading. The risks are greater, and if you do not learn how to manage them, then you may find it extremely difficult to become a successful options trader.

Losses are a reality in trading, just as profits are. The quicker you understand this basic concept, the better able you will be to control your risks. Risk management is a way of ensuring that every trading decision you make is realistic, and your expectations must reflect that.

Thousands of people enter the options market daily to trade, yet the vast majority of them fail to survive for the long haul. Most beginners fail to make it because they simply don't know how to manage their losses. Managing profits is easy, but when losses come around, you are tempted to sit back and wait for the market to even itself out. In most cases, when a new options trader suffers a loss, they adopt the proverbial wait-and-see strategy, which is one of the most terrible things to do when trading options. Without learning how to manage risk, your trading account may suffer irreparable losses.

7.2 Importance of Risk Management to an Options Trader

Almost every single beginner in options trading focuses exclusively on trading strategies. If their strategy fails, they simply give up on it and try to find another approach that will work for them. Options trading, just like other forms of securities, have the risk of the value of the option changing over time. However, the difference is that the value of the option is never linear to the underlying stock. For this specific reason, understanding and predicting the risks linked to trading options is much more difficult.

What you need to realize is that the biggest cause of failure for a new options trader isn't lack of technical knowledge. Even the veteran traders make mistakes. Options trading can be very complex at times, especially if you haven't taken the time to learn how the system works. The biggest problem you face as a beginner is, therefore, failing to adopt a reasonable risk management plan.

Your strategy may be great, but it is not a guarantee that you will not lose money. This is why risk management is an integral part of options trading. As a beginner, learning how to manage risks will help prepare you for more effective trading. There is no such thing as a perfect system, and there never will be. You simply have to learn to manage and control what you have so that you avoid losing every dime you've got.

Here are some of the benefits of knowing risk management:

- Risk management is the biggest factor that determines your success in options trading.

- Risk management enables you to grow your portfolio

- Risk management minimizes the chances of making losses and bad investments.

- Risk management helps you reduce unnecessary risks and control risk exposure.

- Risk management enables you to hedge against volatility in the market.

7.3 Overview of Risk Management for Options Trading

- Risk management can be broken down into a few significant points – Create a trading plan, ensure that the size of your trades is aligned with your risk threshold, learn the pros and cons of your preferred strategy, and have an exit plan.

- Being a successful options trader requires consistency. This involves focusing more on producing above-average results over time rather than aiming for short-term glory.

- Learn how to diversify your portfolio across various asset classes. Even though the majority of your options may be based on stocks, ensure that they are spread out across different sectors of the economy. You should also consider investing in options based on commodities, bonds, and real estate. Diversification minimizes losses and swings during volatile times.

- Never allow your options to exceed 20% of your risk capital.

- Establish stop loss prices and price targets that will favor you.

- Only trade using strategies whose behavior you are comfortable with.

CHAPTER SUMMARY:

1. Risk management involves identifying and assessing your risks so that you can find ways to ensure you make more profits and fewer losses.

2. Risks are a natural part of every options trade. Since there is no way of avoiding them completely, you need to learn how to manage them as effectively as possible.

3. A risk management plan is a tool that you can to minimize your potential risks and increase the chances of making gains. Without it, you might as well be gambling with your money.

4. Stay committed to your risk management plan no matter what happens.

5. When all else fails, always remember these four key points - Create a trading plan; Ensure that the size of your trades is aligned with your risk threshold; Learn the pros and cons of your preferred strategy; and have an exit plan.

YOUR QUICK START ACTION STEP:

We have highlighted some of the steps that you can take to reduce or manage your trading risks. It would be a good idea at this point to attempt to implement one of the risk management strategies.

For example, you could decide to diversify your portfolio. If you are interested in technological stock options, then consider your current financial situation and goals in order to determine how you will spread out your risks. You could invest in different companies, such as Google, Apple, Facebook, etc. At the same time, diversification requires that you put your money in diverse sectors, so also consider investing in financial institutions or industrial firms.

Chapter 8:
Options Trading
Tools

8.1 Overview

Here is an overview of some of the most effective options trading tools that you can use:

Options Pricing Calculator

This tool allows you to research the implied volatility of an option as well as its contract Greeks. The calculator also enables you to predict theoretical values and weigh them against the current bid and ask price. One key advantage of this tool is that it is easy enough even for beginners to understand. The format is intuitive and clear.

Probability Calculator

This tool uses the implied volatility to help you figure out the chances of hitting your targets. The probability calculator helps you determine the probability of being successful when you use a particular strategy.

Profit and Loss Calculator

By using the profit and loss calculator, a trader is able to get a clearer perspective of the profit or loss that their trade will make beforehand. This tool even goes further to show you how the outcome may change depending on volatility and time.

Options and Strategy Scanners

This tool is perfect for finding those trades that match your criteria. You can use the Options Scanner to screen more than 150,000 individual options contracts by choosing the relevant criteria, such as time to expiration, volatility, liquidity, cost, and risk. There is a Basic Search function that enables you to decide which option to trade in based on the above criteria. The Advanced Search function incorporates filters to refine your search further.

The Strategy Scanner helps you identify specific options strategies that align with your preferences. It searches for both basic and complex strategies.

Both these scanners allow you to place a trade within seconds.

Stock, Mutual Fund, and ETF Screeners

Depending on what type of asset class you want to base your options on, this tool allows you to find securities that match your strategies and objectives. You can use a predefined screen or personalize your own. You can screen all your stocks, mutual funds, and ETF options from one place. You can also save your screen whenever you want to.

8.2 Importance of Options Trading Tools

The fundamental importance of using options trading tools is that they make the trading process easier, faster, and less cumbersome. There is no need to resort to using manual techniques that are inefficient and waste a lot of time. These tools help traders to conduct comprehensive research that will potentially help them lower the risk of losses and boost their chances of making a profit.

The general benefits of trading tools include:

- Options trading tools are easy to use because they have predefined selections as part of their configuration.

- These tools also allow you to customize the screen you want to use for your options trading strategy. You can add your criteria, share your strategies with other traders via a network, and even receive notifications when new and matching results appear.

- These tools reduce the hassle of trading by placing all your different investment options in one place.

- These tools help you to make the best trading decision based on your own search criteria.

- The tools can also allow you to trade directly with them. There is no need to move to a different platform to trade your options.

8.3 How to Use Options Pricing Calculators

These are the basic steps for using an Option Price Calculator:

1. Open the Options Pricing Calculator tool.

2. Assuming you want to trade in stock options, just choose the underlying stock symbol. Click on the tab *Stock or Index Symbol.*

3. The pricing calculator will automatically populate the relevant fields.

4. Adjust the variables according to your forecast. You can enter the implied volatility, dividends, interest rate, and expiration. If you wish, you can calculate the implied volatility by factoring in the price of the option.

5. The tool will then provide you with theoretical option values, Greeks for the put and call, and current bid/ask prices.

CHAPTER SUMMARY:

1. Options trading tools are necessary in today's technologically advanced world. You will find trading very cumbersome if you don't learn how to use them.

2. There are several tools that can come in handy when trading in stocks. These include options pricing calculators, probability calculators, profit and loss calculators, options and strategy scanners, and stock screeners. Each tool is important in its own way and has its unique benefits.

3. Trading tools make options trading faster, easier, and more effective. You can get any kind of information you want, wherever you are.

4. Most of the options trading tools are customizable. They allow you to build your own screener according to selected criteria that meet your personal trading needs.

5. In the world of options trading, information is power. However, the right information received at the right time will make you both powerful and rich.

6. Options Pricing Calculators are quite easy to use. From the example above, we have seen that the most important thing is to feed in the right information in the right way.

YOUR QUICK START ACTION STEP:

The trading tools described in this chapter are not difficult to use. You can go online and search for an Options Pricing Calculator that you can use on a free trial basis. Some brokers allow beginners to test their tools for a limited period of time. Alternatively, you can choose any of the other tools mentioned here. Practice makes perfect, so make sure that you go and check out how these tools work.

Chapter 9:
Different Types
of Options

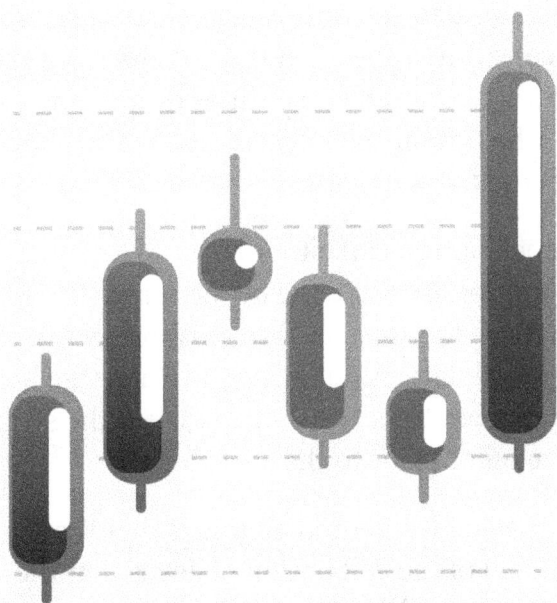

9.1 Overview

When it comes to the trading of options, there are three major categories. These are stock options, binary options, and index options.

Stock Options

Stock options are privileges sold by a party to another, giving the buyer the right, but not the obligation, to sell or buy a stock at a specified price within a specified time. A stock option is a contract between two entities or individuals, and the options usually represent 100 shares of the stock.

A stock option can either be a call or a put. A call option is where the buyer agrees to purchase the stock at the strike price by a specified date. A put option is where the buyer issues a contract to sell the stock at the strike price on or prior to the specified date.

The basic idea behind all this is that the buyer (holder) of the call option believes that the stock price will increase, while the seller believes the price will fall. In the event that the stock price goes up before the contract expires, the option holder benefits because they would have bought the stock at a discount. On the other hand, if the buyer perceives that the stock price will drop, they can issue a put option contract where they are allowed to sell the stock in the future. In case the stock loses value before the expiration date, the option holder has the right to sell off the stock for a premium.

The strike price is the major factor that determines the value of an option. Since it is predetermined, there is a risk involved. The call option holder makes a profit only when the price drops below market value. The put option holder makes a profit only when the strike price rises above the prevailing market price.

It is important to note that employee stock options are a bit different. They do not have a specific date of maturity. In other words, the employee has to stay employed in the company for a specific period before they get the right to buy stock options. Instead of a strike price, employee stock options have a grant price that represents the value of the stock at the time of receiving the options.

Binary Options

Binary options are simple financial assets. They rely on a simple "Yes" or "No" proposal – Will the value of an asset be above a particular price at a particular time? Trades are then made depending on whether the trader believes the answer to be Yes or No. This makes them very appealing to new traders.

However, it is important to understand how they work, the markets involved in binary options trading, and the benefits and risks attached to them. The price is usually set between $0 and $100. There is a bid price and an offer price.

An example of a proposition is this: Will the price of silver be above $1000 at 12:30 p.m. today? If you believe that it will be, then you go ahead and buy the binary option at the offer price. If your answer is No, then you sell at the current bid price, which is usually lower than the offer price. If the price is above$1000 at 12:30 p.m., then the option expires and you make a profit. If the price drops, then you lose everything you bid.

Index Options

These are financial derivatives based on stock indices like the Dow Jones Industrial Average or the S$P 500. An index option gives an investor the right to buy or sell a stock index for a specific period of time.

Index options can be categorized as either American style or European style. With American style options, an investor can exercise at any time prior to expiration. However, European style options can only be exercised when they expire.

Though index options offer similar flexibility and benefits to stock options, they have the added advantage of offering an investor exposure to a wider range of securities. In other words, rather than focusing on the stocks of one company, an index option is based on a pool of stocks from various companies.

Another difference between the index and stock options is that index options are settled by cash and not through deliverables. Finally, an index option usually involves the strike price and premium being expressed in terms of points.

9.2 Importance of Options

The reality is that options can be a bit complex, especially if you have never traded in them before. The three types of options explained above are the most common and you are bound to run into them sooner or later. If you are going to succeed in the field of options trading, you must understand what they are all about and how to handle them.

Every options trader will tell you that stock, binary, and index options have their benefits as well as their inherent risks. The more you learn about them, the better off you will be when it is time to invest or trade in options. This will help you make a decision that will positively affect your bottom line.

Benefits of Options:

Stock Options

- Put options can hedge you from a potential drop in share value.

- They give the option holder enough time to decide whether they will buy or sell the stocks.

- They make the speculation of price movements easier. You can enter into a contract with no obligations whatsoever of exercising the trade options.

- They allow you to diversify your portfolio without investing as much capital as you would when buying shares directly.

- Options trading offer greater leverage because you can profit from a price change without having to pay full price for the stocks.

Binary Options

- The risk is capped, so you cannot lose more than the cost of the trade.

- The payout is already known when investing your money. You will either settle at $100 or lose everything.

- The risk/reward ratio is usually much higher than the underlying asset.

- They are accessible with little capital.

Index Options

- They provide exposure to a wider range of securities than stocks or binary options.

- They provide greater leverage for profits since percentage gains tend to b higher than for the underlying asset.

- They offer protection for your stock portfolio.

9.3 General Steps in Trading options

1. Outlook – You come up with a specific outlook that determines your options strategy. First, you consider the direction of the price movements. Then you consider your price target. Finally, you estimate how long you want to hold

the option for the underlying asset. Accuracy is critical.

2. Planning – Once you have figured out your outlook, you have to decide the options strategy you will use as well as how much money you will commit.

3. Entry – You can trade options outright by writing or buying call or put options. You will need to use the Sell To Open or Buy To Open order.

4. Exit – There are four ways of exiting an options position. You can exercise, assign, roll forward, or close. For the purposes of this book, we shall consider the Exercising option, which means you buy or sell the underlying stock as per the contract.

CHAPTER SUMMARY:

1. Stock options are privileges sold by a party to another, giving the buyer the right, but not the obligation, to sell or buy a stock at a specified price within a specified time.

2. Binary options are simple financial assets that rely on a simple "Yes" or "No" proposal – Will the value of an

asset be above a particular price at a particular time?

3. These are financial derivatives based on stock indices like the Dow Jones Industrial Average or the S$P 500. An index option gives an investor the right to buy or sell a stock index for a specific period of time.

4. It is important for your career or trading success to learn as much as you can about stock, binary, and index options. They are three common types of options that have the potential to make you a lot of profit. However, this can only happen if you know how to handle them

5. When it comes to trading in stock, binary, and index options, you must realize the inherent benefits and risks that each carry.

6. Trading options involve crafting a specific outlook, planning your strategy, entering the market, and then exiting by exercising your options contract.

YOUR QUICK START ACTION STEP:

The information in this chapter can seem a bit overwhelming for a beginner. That is why you should set some time aside to practice what you have learned here. Try the four simple steps outlined in section 9.3. It will help you understand everything better.

Chapter 10: Buying Calls

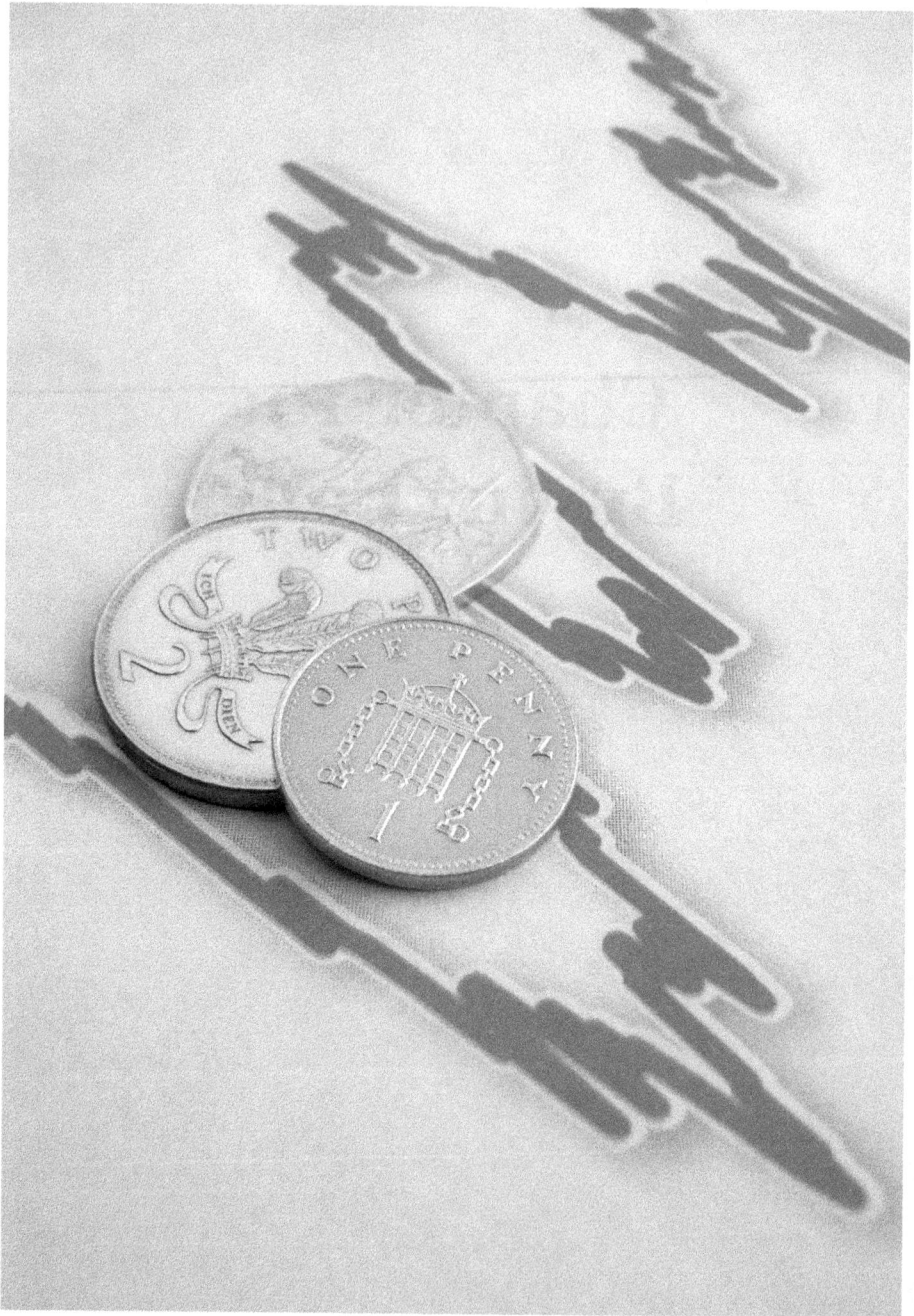

10.1 Overview

We already defined a call as a type of options contract which gives you the right to purchase the underlying stock at the strike price within a specific period of time.

Buying a call option means purchasing an options contract because you believe that the price of the underlying stock will go up. It is a way of profiting from the appreciation of the price of a stock.

By buying a call, you can control the underlying asset and earn a profit when it appreciates in value. However, you will also be able to minimize your losses since the only money that will change hands is the premium you pay to the seller.

Buying call options enable you to maximize your leverage and realize a significant percentage of returns depending on how much capital is invested. You can buy a call if you want to lock in a specified purchase price and yet you don't have the money at that time to buy the security.

There are three things that you will always need to consider when you want to establish a position. The first is your maximum gain. When you have long call position, you benefit from having an unlimited maximum gain. The level of appreciation of the stock price is what determines how much profit you make.

The second is your maximum loss. When you have a long call position, the maximum amount you can lose is what you paid the seller as a premium. Finally, you have to consider your breakeven point. You must ask yourself where the stock price will be when the contract expires. The breakeven is calculated by adding the strike price to the premium.

10.2 Why You Need to Learn About Buying Calls

Does all the information that you have learned so far about buying call options seem a bit confusing? If your answer is 'Yes,' then that's a good thing. That is an indicator of the importance of first acquiring enough knowledge about buying calls before you engage in your first trade.

There are some factors that you must always consider before buying a call option. You have to decide whether you think the stock is going to move up or down. This is important because it determines the kind of options contract you buy. You should only buy a call option if you think the price of the underlying asset will appreciate. Having such kind of knowledge is what will make the difference between success and failure.

There is also the need to be able to predict the level of appreciation or depreciation of the underlying stock. This is what will help you determine the strike price for the options contract you will buy. You don't just pick any random strike price. There are options quotes or chains that you have to base your decisions on. This is another reason why every options trader needs to learn the fundamentals of buying calls.

Finally, there is the time factor. All options contracts have an expiration date. However, you cannot just choose any random date you want. Your decision will depend on the options chain. It can be anywhere from a couple of days to years. As a beginner, it is recommended that you choose a monthly or yearly expiration date.

It should be clear now why a new trader needs to learn how to buy call options the right way. It can get confusing, and there's no need to lose your capital because you decided to kayak downstream without a paddle!

Here are a few benefits of learning how to buy calls:

- You will be able to decide the direction of stock movements.

- You will be able to benefit from a rise in stock prices.

- You will be able to keep your losses down to the amount you paid for the premium.

- You will be able to calculate your breakeven point for long calls.

- You will be able to predict how high or low the price of the stock will move.

10.3 How to Buy Call Options

Now that you have a little bit more understanding about buying call options, let's explore the simple steps that you can follow when buying calls:

1. Find the stock that you believe will appreciate in value.

2. Review the Option Chain for that stock.

3. Choose the expiration date (month) for that particular stock.

4. Choose the strike price.

5. Examine the market price of that call option to determine if it is reasonable.

CHAPTER SUMMARY:

1. Buying a call option means purchasing an options contract because you believe that the price of the underlying stock will go up. It is a way of profiting from the appreciation of the price of a stock.

2. Buying calls can be confusing for a new trader. You need to consider factors such as movement of the stock and its price, as well as the time value of the contract.

3. There are five basic steps to buying call options: Identify your preferred stock, review the option chain, pick the expiry date and strike price, and then check the market to see if the price is reasonable.

YOUR QUICK START ACTION STEP:

Now that you know exactly how to buy calls, you should go ahead and try it. You can easily sign up for a trading account with a reputable brokerage. Start practicing your options trades as soon as possible so that you learn how to become a successful trader. Remember, practice makes perfect!

Chapter 11:
Buying Puts

11.1 Overview

By now we should understand what options are and how they work. We should also know that there are two types of options: Calls and Puts. In this chapter, we shall explore puts and how to buy them.

A put option can be described as an option contract where the option holder has the right to sell an underlying asset at a specific price by a specific deadline. The seller (writer) of the put option has the right to buy the underlying asset at the strike price in the event that the other party exercises their sell option. The seller of the put option usually receives a premium since they are taking on a greater risk.

Traders buy puts if they perceive that the price of the asset will drop. If at the expiration of the contract the stock price happens to be lower than the strike price, then the trader end up making a profit. Their assumption that the value of the stock would fall is proven correct, and they walk away happy and richer.

However, if the stock price rises (contrary to their expectation) above the strike price, then the trader simply allows the contract to expire. The only money they lose is the premium they paid.

In such a transaction, the role played by the premium is quite significant. For instance, let's consider that the strike price is set at $150 and the premium paid is $20. If the market value of stock ends up at anywhere between $150 and $130, will you make a profit? If so, by how much?

The fact is that you will not make any profit in the above scenario. The only way to be assured of a profit would be if the stock price dropped to below $130. In other words, for you to realize a profit, the stock price must be less than your strike price minus the premium you paid. This is the break-even point when buying a put.

There are some important terms that you need to learn here. If the strike price agreed upon is higher than the market price of the stock, the put option is described as being *in-the-money*. In other words, the trader will make a profit.

However, if the market price of the stock is higher than then strike price, then the put option is described as being *out-of-money*. In other words, the trader is going to make a loss by exercising the put options contract. In such a case, you are better off letting the option expire.

There is a third situation that you may find yourself in. It is possible for the market price of the stock to equal the strike price. When this happens, the put option is described as being *at-the-money*.

11.2 Importance of Learning about Buying Puts

When you consider the complexities of buying puts and the different types of trades available (long puts and short puts), you will quickly realize that there are a variety of strategies that you can use. It is critical that you be able to know which strategy will suit you best so that you don't end up confusing yourself and making losses.

In most cases, you would have to consult your broker for more information, but the best way would be to learn it yourself. There are commission fees and transaction costs involved, not to mention tax considerations. Have you thought about any of these factors?

Whatever strategy you pick will be affected in some way by the factors mentioned above. This is why you need to gain enough information and learn about how to buy puts before you actually start trading. It is only through continuous learning that you will increase your knowledge and become a successful trader.

Here are some of the benefits of buying puts:

- Put options offer an attractive way to short stock and make profits when stock prices drop.

- Buying puts allows you to protect your long stock position.

- Put options allow you to protect your unrealized profit.

- The maximum loss you can incur is the cost of the premium

11.3 How to Buy Puts

These are the general steps on how to buy puts:

1. Get permission from your online broker to trade options. This is a simple process and won't cost anything.

2. Choose the stocks or index ETF you want to buy puts on. Make sure the options you buy are liquid.

3. Calculate the number of puts you need to buy. Your broker can provide you with a spreadsheet or some program to do this.

4. Select the expiration date for the options contract. It is recommended that you choose long-term puts.

5. Select a strike price.

6. Purchase the puts by entering an option order through your broker.

CHAPTER SUMMARY:

1. A put option is as an option contract where the option holder has the right to sell an underlying asset at the strike price by a specific expiration date.

2. There are many strategies and factors to consider when trading in put options. For a beginner, this can be complex and confusing. That is why you need to take the time to learn the fundamentals of buying puts.

3. There are six simple steps to buying put options: Get permission from your broker, choose the stock options you want, determine how many put options you need, select the expiration date, pick a strike price, and then enter an options order.

YOUR QUICK START ACTION STEP:

Now that you know exactly how to buy puts, you should go ahead and try it. You can easily sign up for a trading account with a reputable brokerage. Start practicing your options trades as soon as possible so that you learn how to become a successful trader. Remember, practice makes perfect!

BONUS Chapter: Choosing Right Options to Trade

12.1 Factors to Consider

There are so many different strategies that can be used when trading options that most beginners can easily get confused. It, therefore, becomes quite challenging to identify which option to trade. When it comes to choosing the right options to trade, there are a number of factors that you need to consider. These are objectives, risk and reward profile, volatility, events, strategy, and parameters.

When trading in options, you need to have an investment objective. Maybe you want to speculate on a bearish or bullish view of your preferred asset. You could simply be interested in hedging the risks of your stocks or want to earn some income.

The risk/reward payoff is also a factor to be considered because it depends on just how much of a risk you can tolerate. Your appetite for risk will then determine the kind of strategy you are willing to pursue.

It is also important to understand the level of volatility for your options. Take a good look at the volatility of the options you want to trade in and compare them with the historical volatility of the market. This will help you identify the right strategy.

Events are simply incidences or occurrences that have an impact either on a specific stock or an entire market. Whether it is a Federal Reserve announcement or a product launch, events will influence the appropriate expiration date for your options.

Once you have considered the above four factors, you will then have a clearer picture as to what kind of strategy to adopt. This will then lead you to establish your option parameters.

The factors that have been highlighted above are based on particular assumptions. We have assumed that you have already made up your mind as to which financial asset you want to trade using options. You could be interested in trading stocks or ETF options, and maybe your decision was made using a stock screener, fundamental analysis, or 3rd party research.

In any case, we have provided you with above techniques based on the fact that you have already identified your preferred financial asset.

12.2 Importance of Learning How to Choose the Right Options

There are two major benefits that options have. Firstly, they enable you to invest in a wide range of financial instruments, for example, stocks, commodities, ETFs, and others. Secondly, options are so versatile that you can use any trading strategy on them. However, this is where things get complicated for beginners.

With such an extensive range of choices and strategies available, it becomes almost impossible to make a decision. There are simply too many choices that it is easy to get trapped by decision paralysis. For this reason, you have to acquire the necessary knowledge of how to choose the right options to trade in.

You can decide to just close your eyes, hover your finger over all the choices available, and pick at random, but that would be a stupid way of doing things. You do not want to leave your trading success to chance. By learning about the factors that you must consider when choosing the right options, you are making sure that the decision you make is the right one.

The benefits of learning how to choose the right options to trade include:

- It enables you to implement a logical thought process so that decision-making becomes easier.

- It shows you where to start as a beginner when faced with multiple investment options and strategies to use.

- It helps you understand your risk/reward profile better so that you trade according to the strategy that fits an aggressive or conservative trader.

- It helps you understand how the price of an option is set.

- You will be able to maintain an awareness of all the expected events that can potentially affect the volatility and prices of options in the market.

12.3 General Step-by-Step Guide When Choosing Options

So what are the steps involved in the process of picking the right options to trade in?

1. Formulate your investment objective. This forms the foundation for all the following steps.

2. Determine what kind of trader you are i.e. conservative or aggressive trader. The strategy you use in options trading must always align with your risk/reward profile.

3. Examine the degree of volatility in the market in order to gauge options prices.

4. Identify the expected events that may impact the prices and volatility of options.

5. Develop a strategy that fits your objectives, risk appetite, volatility, and key events that may potentially impact the underlying stock.

6. Establish your parameters, for example, strike price, expiration, and option delta. These will determine what kind of call option you go with.

CHAPTER SUMMARY:

1. There are six factors that must be considered when picking the right options to trade. They include your trading objectives, risk tolerance, volatility, expected events, strategy, and parameters.

2. The six factors mentioned above are based on the assumption that you have already decided on the financial instrument you want to trade using options.

3. Beginners are faced with a wide array of choices due to the benefits that options have. In order to avoid getting stuck in making a decision, it is important to

educate yourself on how to choose the right options to trade. By considering the factors above, you put yourself in a better position to make the right choice.

4. There are six key steps in the process of picking the right options to trade. These steps are linked to the factors that were considered in the beginning.

YOUR QUICK START ACTION STEP:

The information provided in this chapter is by no means exhaustive. As a beginner who wants to learn how to trade options, you need to develop a thirst for continual knowledge. We recommend that you visit one of the many websites that can provide you with additional information. A good place to start would be www.investopedia.com.

Conclusion

Thank you again for owning this book!

I hope this book was able to help you to understand the fundamentals of buying and selling stock options. This book has provided you with an introduction to the world of options trading and how to build a foundation that will launch you into success.

The next step is to take the knowledge you have gained here and put it into practice. It would be futile to read through all these pages only to fail to take the required action. Go back to the end of every chapter and use the Quick Start Action Steps to test yourself and see how far you can go. I am sure that it won't be long before you discover that options trading is challenging, fast-paced, and potentially rewarding!

Thank you and good luck!

About the Author

Warren Richmond is a professional trader and investment professional of 10 years.

When he was in college, he got interested in trading and investing early but got frustrated understanding the highly complex topic.

Warren wanted a teaching method that he could easily learn from and develop his trading and investing skills. He soon discovered a teaching series that made him learn faster and better.

Applying the same approach, Warren successfully learned the necessary skills in order to become a professional trader and is now teaching the subject matter through writing books.

With the books that he writes on trading, he hopes to provide great value and help readers interested to learn trading.

www.ingramcontent.com/pod-product-compliance
Lightning Source LLC
Chambersburg PA
CBHW071432210326
41597CB00020B/3755